Lunar wake

Lunar wake

Catherine Hunter

Turnstone Press

Turnstone Press
607-100 Arthur Street
Winnipeg, Manitoba
Canada R3B 1H3
www.TurnstonePress.com

Turnstone Press gratefully acknowledges the assistance of The Canada Council for the Arts, the Manitoba Arts Council and the Government of Canada through the Book Publishing Industry Development Program for our publishing activities.

Some of these poems have appeared in *Prism International*, *Contemporary Verse 2*, *Prairie Fire* and *NeWest Review*. The epigraph by Rainer Maria Rilke to "afterlife" is taken from the translation by Steven Mitchell. The epigraph by Osip Mandelstam to "Castaway" is taken from the translation by W.S. Merwin and Olga Carlisle.

Cover art: "Night Scene-Scream" by Michael Olito, 1975

Cover design: Michael Olito

Text design: Manuela Dias

This book was printed and bound in Canada by Hignell Printing for Turnstone Press.

Second printing: March, 1998

Canadian Cataloguing in Publication Data

Hunter, Catherine, 1957–

Lunar wake

Poems.
ISBN 0-88801-184-9

I. Title.

PS8565.U5783L8 1994 C811'.54 C94-920215-0
PR9199.3.H8578L8 1994

this book is for
George Morrissette

Acknowledgements

Special thanks to George Amabile for his criticism and his encouragement, and to Mike Olito for his fabulous collage.

Many thanks also to Kate Bitney, who turned over the cards; to Debbie Cygman, who took me, quite against my will, to the casino; and to Melody Morrissette, who interrupted.

These poems were written during time provided by a grant from the Manitoba Arts Council.

Table of Contents

"Life, he himself said once . . . is a wake"
—James Joyce

Getting rid of the moon

Gender relations

the moon is a woman (of course) and the man
in the moon is a transvestite, cloaking himself
in her silver clothes; or the moon is pregnant
and the man in the moon is her baby, rocking himself
in her high, gold womb
                                        or maybe the moon
is a ventriloquist
the man in the moon is her puppet
she carved him out like a jack-o'-lantern
she hides her heavy woman's body with a mask

I've heard that the sun
is male, possibly holy, followed by sun dogs,
man's best friend, burning himself
out very gradually, carefully, always retreating
whenever she comes around

there's no woman
                              in the sun
too hot, perhaps, or perhaps
a woman can't get inside a man the way a man
can get inside a woman, burrowing there
and taking root, hollowing her out
until he swallows her whole,
grins like a cat
                         and maybe I want you
inside me, maybe I remember

you said the moon could float in the Pacific Ocean
and you had some scientific explanation why she doesn't
but I think it's simply that she can't exist down here
where everything is split in two and can't change colour
except those rare times we
surround each other

when we love

dancing the waves, no longer caring
why we sing or who

we're singing for

Crabapple

the crabapple tree sheds
bruised white petals,
tight red fruit as hard as bullets

when you bite, your mouth goes dry
you remain innocent

the crabapple tree stretches
up to the second storey
in case of fire

it hides you from your brothers
in its broad green leaves

at twilight, it coaxes the moon
to settle in its branches
but the moon is high
and hard and willful

it's not coming down
for anything

it says, probably sour anyway

this is where the first kiss
occurs, right beneath
your mother's window

all winter, the crabapple tree
hangs heavy with snow,
remembering

and in April, this is where
you find a silver dollar
in your dreams, you spend it
again and again

but your mother cannot sleep
she opens her curtain and leans
into the night

she sighs, a pale green
haze appears above the tree,
descends upon the upper limbs,
as light as breath

Moon poem for Irene

at night the telephone poles
blossom in the dark the operator
doesn't know the lines escape and stretch
themselves for free above the prairies
foothills orchards yes a kind of sentence
that unravels over mountains lakes the broken
cities all receivers opening
like petals or like knifeblades
can't you hear it bouncing
off the satellites a silver buzzing
revolution of the voice

reading of the man who had a telephone
installed inside his coffin I was thinking
of the time we talked all night and
how at dawn we finally drifted into sleep
our two dreams rambling on and still
connected to each other   listen
when the sun goes down it's possible
to pluck the moon and drop it
in the slot the company's been
overthrown the night is young the bird
is waiting on the wire there's a clear path
through the air waves all the way
across the country   call me

Beauty*

the bride of Frankenstein's monster is rising
she has pushed off the weights that held her underwater
she floats like baby Moses in her basket
patchwork arms and legs, a broken heart
and stitched-up stomach, one eye crumpled
like a cracked egg in her closed palm

she feels no pain, but asks for her two fathers
where is the man who wanted someone
hideous as himself? the man who wove
and then unwove her?
all she can hear is the water
she cries to it with her bent mouth,
not knowing the word *mother*

perhaps there is a prayer for those
who have been created second,
dismembered, cast adrift,
but she is ignorant of prayer

the moon could be an apple,
for all she knows

she bites it
with her one
open eye

* *"The remains of the half-finished creature, whom I had destroyed, lay scattered on the floor . . . and I accordingly put them into a basket, with a great quantity of stones, and, laying them up, determined to throw them into the sea that very night."*

—Mary Shelley, *Frankenstein*

Werewolf

the werewolf, trapped
in the pale subjunctive,
paints her nails a delicate
tea-pink coral, singing along
with the radio: *I fall to pieces*

sometimes she grows nostalgic
for her seven husbands
she reads the labels
on her lipstick: lilac,
frosted honey, nectarine
she brushes and brushes
and brushes her hair

she walks to the post office,
wearing sunglasses, collects
her unemployment cheque
and reads the headlines on a women's magazine
offering cures: avoid caffeine and alcohol
and salt, especially salt

she remembers the desperado, oh
of all the husbands, he was her favourite
the bravest one, the one who lasted longest
sometimes she feels like a little round hole
on a telephone dial
with twenty-eight numbers
she looks in the mirror, bares her teeth and says
if I were beautiful if I were rich if I were
someone else, and like a ferris wheel
the month moves on, the moon
is always dialing
zero

Moon poem for Patrick

here you come walking again
balanced on the telephone wire
holding the rent for that one room
in your bare hands

who cares if the shoe drops
off, the socks unravel
and the bones of the feet won't knit?

someone comes rising up at the window,
just as you're counting
your last candles,
and visits you

Harvest moon

driving home over the backroads we saw two deer
standing with their necks bowed one across the other
as though they had grown careless and sleepy with fear

you told the story of Diana at her bath
how she could turn a man into an animal
antlers sprouting from his head like young, mute trees

we lit a fire in the garden after midnight
the scarecrow watched the fatted moon
and dreamed of melons, squash, fruition

and decay; all night you told me tales
of archery and love, our bodies bent
together in a kind of repetition

the way two boxers lean against each other
in the ring, until they're forced apart
and must begin their work again

Hunter's moon

last night I dreamed that I performed so many deeds
and was so beautiful and brave,
they named the moon after me

911

who knows how many
lives I've saved? I'm a hero
a bone bridge over thin ice, a bondsman
at the cemetery gate, a fire escape,
a two-lipped pump for the cramped lung, dancing
mouth to mouth with the young soldiers

or the time I climbed that telephone pole
on Catherine Street, to catch
a damaged aircraft in my gentle hands

perhaps you've seen me on the avenue
swaggering in my baby shoes
a winged horse at my shoulder
and all the drunken children of the city
gathered in a wreath
around my neck

A live audience

I was filmed before a live audience
I was stereophonic, in colour, 3D
writing poetry before the television set late
in the morning drinking scotch from a plastic cup
no matter what happened to me I lived through it
mud slides, heat waves, scandal, I cleaned
myself until I glistened, festooned
every limb with jewellery, my lipstick
was the colour of begonias
I paid no attention to what I was writing

I was arrested and pled guilty with my eyes closed
dreaming I was a juvenile and the country
rallied round me waving flags as I confessed
to everything, adultery, plagiarism, envy
every fever and addiction known to man
I was awarded a golden medal, read
every book in the library, swam the Channel
without a bathing suit O let me at the graveyard
with my grappling hook I can raise them up
again to taste the sun I was filmed
before a live audience my two arms
lifted high above my head while the citizens
chanted, victory, victory

Undead poem

my friend Tim with his long eyeteeth
painted fluorescent orange
how he could undo me
at thirteen
under a black light
on Hallowe'en

I used to be scared
of those who returned

now I'm afraid of those
who won't

I offer my
neck, but they rest
easily, apparently
and will not come back

1/2

the bare stick that held the scarecrow leans
toward the frozen ground, bereaved
the pumpkin sags, teeth caved in
like a mad crone, smelling of seed,
brain, a stub of wax
the eyes stained black

something wipes away the moon
with a clock hand
the arm of a compass
between the harvest and the hunter's phase
splits darkness and light

draw the moon on a sheet of paper
cut it in half
erase it

did you think that it would stay away?
it rises over the stockyards
only the birds believed that it was leaving
how they raised their innocent voices in farewell

Moon poem for Z

(

a golden hook, it catches
at the skin

o

a round bone in the throat
see how you stutter
your own face among the stars

***

a lover who won't be turned away
insists upon the beauty of madness
and longing, letters through your mail slot
when you change the locks, tyrannical
and lyrical and swollen with bright
tenderness, remembering his fingers
on your thigh, following you
everywhere
all your life you have been reading
of this, Catherine and Heathcliff crying out
beyond their own deaths
cats in the alley
dogs howling at the yellow hole in the sky
his fingers
on your skin, five pale bruises blooming
underneath the sleeve

the night you came home to find your door open
heat seeping out into the night
                                        nothing stolen only
notations scribbled on your calendar *full tonight*
and once in a while blue
                              you don't want
to be orbited any more
by this soft glowing thing, changing its shape
with every mood and weather
                                      a hook, a bone
it has no shame, obsessed
carnivorous thing
                          without a brain

Getting rid of the moon

though they planted a flag there
and stabbed it through, it lives still

I imagine committing the crime myself
my fingerprints on the typer
a chalk circle in the sky
marking the scene
and would the revolutionaries
praise me at last, would I enter history
would you love me without this
endless maddened grief

the Tarot reader pulls the Priestess from the deck
shows me how she's tamed the moon
a docile crescent underneath her foot
make friends with the moon, she says

the moon grins with its cut mouth
its light shines through to my bones

Regret

I began to regret having made
the moon the way I did
so high, so fickle, so belligerent
at times
            peering through the window
reading Walt Whitman
over my shoulder
                        turning the pages
before I was ready

I believe it was gossiping
people began to say that I was
unsophisticated, mutable, in love
that I believed in beauty and celebrity
that I read Walt Whitman, secretly
at night
            I lay in your bed, white light
coating my body, thinking of fertility
things were getting altogether far too risky

I looked at my shelf of books
the word had infiltrated every page
even the book of the dead instructed:
passion and fear are optical illusions
like the moon in water and I knew
what I had to do

so when you look upon the empty sky, remember
vengeance is mine, I give
and I take away, and after all
it was a case of self-defense,
the moon or me

Lunar wake

I did feel guilty at the funeral of the moon
though I dug my knife and fork in
like everybody else
                                        and it was tasty
little chunks of cheese stabbed through
with little flags, yellow wine to wash it down

the night, of course, was very dark
the wolves and astronauts were inconsolable
Kotex executives wept openly, and mystery writers
came clean, admitting there was nothing
without solution after all: everything was obvious

the earth grew fat and prone to drunkenness,
like an actor who has lost his following
the sea stood still, and when I saw my former husband
he looked just like any other man

I dance on the naked planet at dawn
arms raised in vindication, crowing
everything's perfect, except
the sun's in my eyes
and it's starting
                                 to piss me off

afterlife

"And being dead is hard work"
—Rilke

afterlife

my skeleton does not mourn
the lost muscle, nor the tongue
it rattles its white joy
like a child out of school

barefoot and with empty pockets
bald and picked quite neat
it chatters and rocks until midnight
no longer envies the black sky at bedtime

the stars tick, irregular
as broken clocks

the page lies happy
spare and lean at last and quiet
as a bone

afterlife (2

no trailing clouds, no kite tail
dangling glory, bereft of navel
the skeleton contemplates only
that one hole at the edge
of the horizon, the one mouth
that swallowed the moon

the skeleton dances, crazy
as a puppet with a severed string
unwatched, unwanted, reeling out
and out across the desert floor
the awkward ankles click
like dice, the shoulder blades
shrug off the weight of clay

afterlife (3

on the third day, my skeleton sadly discovers
it has not shed everything

rain water gathers in the wide scoop
of the pelvis, and the birds
still have more wings than humans do

I have not paid the ferryman enough
or else I disembarked too early

the earth persists, a memory scuttles
like a mouse in the blank skull
the skeleton turns its brittle neck
toward home

afterlife (4

the water is broken, the passage
not wholly amnestic and clean

the skeleton sits cross-legged
elbow dangles at the kneecap
head bobs on the clumsy spine
gawking at the way that light unravels
everywhere, those two suns following
each other, like twins
who can't be parted for a day

the skeleton squints and peers
at the shadow hanging
off the bone like cobwebs
the chalk jaws crack
and separate and utter
baby talk

afterlife (5

in a cape and black wires
the skeleton enters the city
wanders beneath the tall buildings
searching for its name, a place to rest

lead me to lie down beside the waters
of the plaza fountain, let the wind sing
through the thin harp
of the ribcage, set a hat
open on the pavement
and wait

the stupid sockets
are still hungering

afterlife (6

my skeleton revisits the scarecrow and the snowman
notes how their bodies are rounded with human care
though no one brings them gifts, the stones and flowers
people lay with sorrow over these rough sticks

my skeleton is not certain, really, what it wants
but it's afraid it wants
the same old things I always wanted
take them yourself, say the ghosts, *that's what we do*
they haunt their former lovers without mercy

but the skeleton cannot do this thing
it has no soul, and nothing to make noise with
except these joints: it creaks past your bed
endlessly, making a sound that you
and your wife believe is the wind
or the house "settling," as you put it,
in your ignorance

my skeleton visits the casino

the roulette table is a small city
hopscotch and coloured parking lots
lopped-off chimney stacks, a brass rail
like a railway track
my skeleton gambles the contents
of its begging bowl nightly
thigh like a pool cue, leaning on the green dark felt
hip like the handle of a crutch, merely leaning
and whether advisable or ill-advised, it clacks
the chips against each other, taunting the other players
because what they lose, they can lose
once only, while the skeleton knows
a delicious repetition of loss

over by the slot machine
a woman rolls a cigarette with one hand
counting up lemons and cherries, her lips
flecked with tobacco, she looks out the window
and there in the sky is her last dime, ripe
and waiting to be spent, the one coin
she can never quite get rid of

Castaway

"because the soul is a woman and fond of trifles"
—Osip Mandelstam

☪

reading the book of the dead
no longer understanding language
the way it promises
to chase away the seven dogs

the way it warns
against the hungry ghosts as if
you could ward off their yellow light

with simple words
which after all are only prayers

the sounds a sightless woman makes
when she moves through the strange halls
of a building for the first time

or a bird trying over and over
to enter the greenhouse

I did my time, stayed after school
stood in the corridor, a ruler
balanced on my head

I wrote one hundred sentences
exactly alike

and still, nothing prepared me

for this loss of meaning,
this punishment

☪

naming, like a mantra
every place you walked
the beach the boat the sea the garden

a room where a book lies open
on the staircase and the wind
turns the pages

as though the reader had gone
for a drink of water,
neglecting just this once
to mark his place

☪

one string from your guitar
the A, coiled and split
on the closet floor

a drawing of fire
rolled up into a cylinder
and held together
with a loose white knot

the fingerprints you left
on every surface in the house

☪

why invest these cast off objects
with such longing
and devotion

these empty hands
their white bracelets

this cottage on the lip of the cove
its walls blown clean by rain

a wide arc along the shoreline
where the tide recedes and disappears

where only a fool
would stand after nightfall

her mouth wide open, breathing
the dark salt air

☪

remembering a poem by Osip Mandelstam
in which Psyche is bewildered
stepping down into the shade
not recognizing where she is

she won't let go
of the useless coin she hides
in her fist

she walks without seeing
holding a mirror before her face

her warm, invisible breath
clouds the glass

☪

these white circles at the wrist
ears with their golden hoops
as though the body knew
what was to come, adorned itself
with the sign for zero, in preparation

the way a woman who expects her husband
will sprinkle her wrists
with rose oil after a bath, lie down
in the middle of the afternoon
pretend to sleep

flowered sheets, a candle flame
wind still blowing
into the room

☪

one white moonshell on a kitchen shelf
a sugar bowl, the dry pods of a poppy
remain what they are
cannot be conjured into stories

the salt foam gathers in a narrow rim
a curve recording how the tide pool
overflows and empties

the way a dream condenses in the morning
and sinks back inside the body

I wrap myself inside your clothing
walk outside all night above the beach

☪

are you naked now, are you forgetting
all things falling swiftly from you
like the melted wax of wings, the book,
the drawing, the guitar, my own
discarded body, broken, washed away

like that painting of the nameless saint
ascending through the thunderclouds
his robes unravelling toward earth

a man the shape of flame, the shape
of a tornado

☪

there were times I did not want
to be entered

times I asked for this

the silent rush of blood
into the vacuum
of the heart

what we might be hearing
when we cup a seashell
to each ear, or when we bow our heads
below the snow line in the winter

a sound that always came in at the window
whenever you left the house
or when you stopped singing

☪

returning always to the things
that you have touched
watercolour water in a jar
an unwashed brush

tell me, is the soul so frivolous
is this what it wants

a woman at heart, after all
begging for trinkets

☪

a woman gazing at her own reflection
until each feature vanishes in fog

one by one they slip beneath the surface
the way the sky absorbs the stars at dawn

and light lands all around me
in the garden

the texture of your worn blue
shirt against my skin

Why I came to live in St. Boniface

Insomnia

entering Regina, 4 a.m.
over the city of my birth
the widow of the moon hangs
clock-faced, impatient
I let my book fall, thinking:
this might be a good place to begin

can never sleep beside you
blood tick-tocking through your veins
lungs exhaling and exhaling
can't let go of you
or when I'm moving away from you
    I never drive, just
        give my body up to the long trains
            and though they rock me, I lie awake
or when I'm finally absent
from you, speaking your name
over wires, counting my dollars
like sheep, adding the price
of a ticket, then I can't sleep

counting up lies, mistakes, omissions,
the many things I can't believe in,
those stories of near-death, bright phantoms
rising over the flesh—what is it
that departs and then returns?

sleep, after all, is a kind of reading
(and this is a love poem, a lullaby)
a journey you must trust, travelling
between the lines, committing
the crime of all passengers: moving
without moving
lying under sheets, under stars
     not the moon but what the moon
          leaves behind
                a soft shred, retained
thinking: here, this might be
the one good place to let go,
coming toward you

Why I came to live in St. Boniface

because it was summertime
you played the fiddle
a cat lay over your doorsill, dreaming
she was neither inside nor out

because you filled the house with jazz
and with tomatoes—the bright sound
of their ripe skins bursting, the scent
of peanut oil

because you concealed from me the fact
that the walls of your house are an illusion
that butterflies and squirrels move through them
that a kitchen ladle can find its way
down to the lilac roots at the bottom of the garden
with no help from a human hand

because you didn't tell me about the wind
how it lets in everything, dead leaves, spiders,
absent-mindedness, the mist off the river

I thought you said you lived
by the sane river

you'd lie beside me on the bed, turn your face
to the wall and see the seven directions
of the neighbourhood, every yard on the street,
bulbs under the grass, the sky

you saw our daughter and you
picked up your fiddle, you baked bread
you brewed beer, you danced
the dance of conspiracy, seduction, *the house*
you said *will make room* and I joined in
we chanted *room room room* the rafters parted
like pelvic bones, door frames bulged outward
our daughter turned her unborn head, listening

we didn't tell her
about the wind

Naming you *(poem interrupted by my daughter)*

the mind is in the trees
that must be a song
my daddy's playing
always in the upper reaches
of the green leaves, tangled
in the white clouds, rippling
like a heat wave, a mirage
among the dippers and the animals
and twins
that's where the man
with the cheese head
lives

impossible to name the mind

and when our daughter came to us we did not
think of naming, we thought only breathe
and breathe and

if you're talking about my dad,
that's true

breathe

he always has crazy things
to say
inside his head

the mind in the trees
floating up above us, as the cheese head floats
above our bodies, bobbing there
like a balloon a child holds
on the celebration of the day of birth
what I was going to talk about,
the day of naming

21 December

nothing but a peach and a pear
two lone receptacles of summer
heavy and pale in the dark
northern kitchen

a baseball forgotten
underneath the table
unravels at its leisure

I am counting everything
that is rounded, curved
like the sun

the green iris of the cat, the o
of the typer, a loose, black
button, your face, your face
wholly mine in these last
moments of sleep

Good Friday

there is no reason to wake up
both of your parents are reading
you lie with open hands and watch
them, two great strangers motionless
in their chairs; if you stare long enough,
they will dwindle and grow flat, as if
seen from a long distance
through a telescope

your father is reading Dostoevsky,
but you can't know this yet
when his mouth droops,
you believe he is disappointed
in his small family or in what he is tasting
as he drinks from a metal cup

you inhale the coffee, it smells
of warm earth and then you remember
the seeds you planted yesterday
with your mother—marigolds,
lobelia, poppies, watermelon—
you slide from your bed to look

the peat pots are silent and dark
their little flags of letters perch
foolishly on their pencils, giving nothing
and the soil is impenetrable, absorbed
as your mother's face
everything in the house settles
and is suddenly solid,
pulled toward the centre of gravity,
that book in her hands

Cat and eggs

the cat lies on the kitchen table
sprawled against the open box of eggs
blinking at the daffodils, conning the sun

you think that you should write a moon poem
for Verla because the eggs
of her chickens are so
mysterious, magnificent
their lunar surfaces
catch the morning light
and hold it there
like some impossible
drawing lesson, like pleasure
you imagine it brims
in the cup of your hand

two of the eggs are small, misshapen, dappled
almost green
like two dark river stones
two jewels your daughter found
when Verla took her out
among the grass and horses
and the gravestones and the bell
that rang across the snow
so long it sounded through to summer

sometimes you feel so grateful
you become simple, you become silly
as though at any moment you might
rise through the air
like a delicate, air-blown shell
and orbit the earth

sometimes you feel the winter
is not going to give you anything
like this again, and then it does:
a cat, a dozen eggs, a sheaf
of yellow flowers

Cat and tomato

the cat,
oblivious as usual
to culture,
ignores the wooden
sidewalks with their
seed-packet street signs
and crawls in a fantastic jungle

in the afternoon
a tail curls out
beneath the cabbage
animal vegetable

she sniffs at a green tomato
larger than her head

lean against
the rusty shovel
and imagine
grass blades blooming
to your shoulder
how once you too were
small enough and wild
and loved disorder

Non/attachment

reading Sri Ramakrishna in the garden
turning the thin, dust-scented
pages *O mother make me desireless*
the rain clouds are not rain clouds,
but illusion, your head against my knee
my bare leg in the ticklish, temporary grass
reading that all pain is rooted
in our foolish love of maya
our brown and flammable daughter
planting lettuce, the moving shadows
of the thunderheads like dark green waves
beneath her feet

I know I have believed you,
Sri Ramakrishna, that this whole bright veil
will burn and shatter, that we sorrow
if we cannot learn dispassion
I am listening to the coming storm,
breathing in the sweet
electric air and I surrender, saying
that if you are right, I will agree
to suffer

Cat and avocado

the cat is happy
watching me slice the green black skin
of the avocado, split it open
the geraniums send out
little flames on the windowsill

today at this table I worked
with a young woman
who birthed four children
before she learned the alphabet

we laboured over sentences
the sunlight fell in broken
colours on the paper
words began to group themselves
like fish swimming together or
geese migrating in wide formations
of grace and we laughed

it is not impossible to feel light
spreading through the body
the cat is happy
licking the pale yellow flesh
of the avocado, licking the sun

while I become metaphorical, insubstantial,
drinking beer from a clean glass, saying
it is not impossible to feel light

The anti-gravity machine

you are eight years old
you are building an ark
out of cardboard and glue
for the mountain gorillas
who live in the clouds
the incalculable white beasts
roaming the arctic circle
the cheetahs, fastest
animals on earth

you are inventing the stars
out of tinfoil, a bedsheet
firmament, volcano
of baking soda and salt
you breathe on the cardboard animals
you set them adrift

upstairs the neighbour tells his wife
that he will throw her off the roof
if she doesn't shut her face
he breaks a bottle and green glass
comes tinkling down outside
your window, emerald hail

you are building an anti-gravity machine
out of paper clips and magnets
see how the white string hangs
in the air
from nothing

Being rich

every man in the neighbourhood has heard
that I have money

they arrive on my doorstep, bearing gifts,
excuses, extra zucchini from their gardens,
empty cups that they want filled with sugar

all day long the telephone rings
every vase in the house is fat
with stolen flowers

the leaking roof is sealed, the doorknobs oiled
every screw sits in its place, exact and tight
the mailbox stands upright and full of letters

my lawn is mowed and watered daily
my bicycle tires are round and plump
I float down the street, pink ribbons
streaming from my hair I'm rich

and happy, every man in the neighbourhood
knows that I have money
they line up at the door,
their little caps in hand,
and kiss me

The flooding

under the norwood bridge, Daniel writes
Daniel loves Catherine
and under the main street bridge,
Brian writes *Brian loves Catherine*
and all summer long
it rains without stopping

the red river sprawls across its banks, swollen and drunk
and faintly reptilian
the assiniboine rises, swallowing everything
graffiti, footpaths, docks, the tops of trees

the garden cannot stop growing
it steams with mosquitoes,
gives birth to a multitude of slugs
they lie curled and glistening,
dark wet pearls among the cabbage leaves
the zucchini wraps its bristling limbs
around the scarecrow, choking him
tickling his bare, washed face
he dreams of sleeping beauty's castle
how everyone suffered the one curse, such unfairness
his legs and feet disintegrate, he smells
the rich green smell of straw and rotting spinach
nothing blooms but the red begonias
and the two-storey onions, their white burst flowers
everywhere like stars

this is what happens when you love
two men at the same time
the sky opens, the earth fills up with water
and the villagers banish you, finally
they cast you out the way the citizens of Thebes
cast out their sinners to remove the plague

you pack your meager things
you paddle your canoe out through the garden
trout are jumping in the corn,
catfish in the small potato patch
you wave good-bye, you see your two men
standing on the two bridges, holding two
umbrellas like bright flags above their heads

you take one last look at your city
its towers of commerce
burnt cathedrals, all submerged
you trail your fingers through the water
gathering algae, braiding a crown for your own head
you enter the wide circle of the floodway, singing

you will become the queen of the mississippi,
queen of the amazon, your throat full of tears
wherever you go with your double heart,
the clouds converge, the forests and jungles
explode with colour, a lush, erotic confusion
and rivers overflow to praise your beauty

you are sorrowful and unrepentant
you are the queen of the nile
your people have sent you into exile

in their dreams, a sparrow appears
with a blue bouquet of flax in her beak
she flies toward the great, ruined city

The electric daughter

all winter in your daughter's bedroom
the air thickens with ions
she lies on the bed,
brooding over long division,
friendship and betrayal
she strokes the cat
fur crackles
underneath her fingers

when you turn out the light
she lifts her arms
to reach your face,
her nightgown shedding
temporary stars
each time she moves
her kiss,
the prick of a needle
on your lip

you shake out the bedclothes
and the green blanket ripples above her
bright with phosphorescence in the dark room

you can't absorb what you see in that moment
long legs, the sudden, unmistakable shape
of a woman there on the sheet

all night you dream of angry honey bees
swarming in a cloud outside your lighted window

meanwhile, the electric daughter
sleepwalks
through the house, gold sparks
falling from her hair
like rain

everything she touches
hurts her

Happyland park

that's the true unbelievable name of the place
traffic circles us and holds us captive

a man on the slant bank
eyes the children playing
a housecat stalks a robin

myself on a bench with a pencil,
the ripped envelope of a government cheque, an idea
that won't light
some days you can't catch anything
the black trees stretch their arms, trying to pull the sun
down through the clouds
three boys are fishing in the creek
the green turtles keep slipping
past their open nets

some days it is impossible to measure
the distance between one body
and another
one girl and another
passing through the pink blurred wall
of a moving rope, singing double dutch songs
weaving in and out as if they weren't afraid
of being caught

The meaning of the dream

I dream that I'm carrying a corpse home from Alberta
in a green wooden coffin that folds in two
like a magic box, with handles and a window
so the face looks out like a drowned face in an aquarium
I dream that my brothers and my friends' brothers
are drunk and won't help me
I drag the coffin onto trains and buses,
heave it onto luggage racks, pull it like a sled
across the road, drop it accidentally
down a flight of subway stairs, while the brothers
make toasts and joke, and the face
of the dead man bumps against the glass
open-eyed and bruised and looking a little
like Frankenstein's monster, now surely
this is a dream worthy of analysis

you suggest that I'm afraid
of travelling, tired of carrying burdens
through traffic, of being abandoned
or that I attend to my dead too often
and inadequately, but I think
the meaning of the dream lies in the drinks
the brothers carry in their hands,
the sparkle and the fizz above each glass
how they forget death: easily, completely
it rises like a bubble and disperses
in the thin, blue air

Penance

Poem to be read in Winnipeg

Mars ascending, again
Orion spitting his white coins
to mark every deathday and birth
with his insufferable northern energy

here on the east side of the seine,
where the names of the saints
peal down every street,
in this transparent, freckled house
I'm always writing out of,
my dead friends come to reclaim me

they will not let me cross,
though the green footbridge lies open
to the city, the river
frozen, the round window
of the burnt cathedral
wide and broken like a second moon
I could skate right through

all winter, while the power company
calculates my debt, the friends are speaking to me

they speak of the city, how it glitters
at night like shattered glass, how easy it is
for the body to lie down there
they say that the city forgets
very quickly, that it is cold

so cold the stars are scraping
against the sky
Orion rises over the river
he sharpens his arrowheads
he looks for the lost sister under the ice

Runaway poem

every day since your birthday the fog
has been thick and bitter
your brothers have been sent to look for you
they pass a cigarette, one to the other
under their tented palms

smoking in the rain, waiting on the corner
at the drugstore with the neon sign that is dying
only the S remains, a short spark
stuttering blue into the street –

they are so still that a crow lands
on the pavement between them,
ruffles its wet, black feathers
one of the brothers opens his mouth
as if to speak

all these movements are so textured, practised
the two brothers stand inside a cloud
breathing cloud breath, waiting

at the back of your jaw
you can feel the extra tooth with your tongue
you are not thinking of your brothers
your left-handedness
or that small slur of a birthmark
at the nape of your neck

the family can't trace its own path
in blood or rain or writing
and the body can't will itself to stay together
how long can the cupped hand hold water
or the throat stay closed? we are always
opening and parting like two
wings, two lips, your father's arm
against my arm, the edge
that breaks desire from desire

and in the summer how the fire bleeds
between the fingers, though the hand's
held firmly up against the sun

Moon again

8:30 in the morning
hoarfrost on every branch and twig
the moon full and white
above the hospital
its blue lakes the colour of sky

spent all night getting rid of the moon
and here it hangs, though its voice
is hoarse in the morning
and I think it has slipped a bit,
tilted, the face dips slightly
toward the earth, perhaps I
wounded it

***

I am walking to obey my handsome doctor
who believes that a person
can will herself whole
holding the X-rays
in his delicate, long fingers,
he says desire
is the strongest medicine

under the two bridges
where the two rivers meet
twenty pigeons circle out on
wings the colour of cold water
city workers flood the ice
for skating, silver winter rain
against the white trees

***

the very end of main street, a red light,
cars steaming like horses, a five-year-old
in bedroom slippers running from the store
with a bag of milk

two girls holding rags against their faces
letting out breath that rises like smoke
thin legs numb in the tight
black stockings, selling things
that don't belong to them

***

this is where they found the newborn
here among the evening papers
swaddled in stories of murder, blue
yet somehow capable of life

this is where the veterans marched
the legion of the war-blinded, drums,
the words of men, that habit they have
of getting holes in them, remembering
how the boys burst open on the beach
how the boys keep falling
through their dreams, the strange, unholy
way we use the word *survival*

***

my doctor loves me, he believes
you can have what you want
if you learn to want; he said
to imagine a heart like fire
a red muscle burning and beating
every cell angry with health

but I think we are all too tired
I can feel it on every corner
every street I cross, streets
that are named for saints and streets
that are named for crooks and streets
with innocent names like Ruby
and Stella and Gertrude, weary women
who just want to get the supper
on the table
before the moon comes up

***

the baby was a girl
remember Daisy crying: *I hope she'll be a fool!*
a little fool
wrapped in paper like a piece of fish
and the moon was no doubt shining
when her mother laid her down
among the parked cars and the garbage
the moon looked on

***

being born is the easy part, yes
it is this staying here that's difficult
this walking for the heart without being certain
exactly why, threading a path through the city
as though I could gather these streets
and bridges to me, hold them in this moment
shining, unassailable

***

what shall we learn to want

let's ask for something possible
that our children will reach out their hands
to the stranger, that when they step into the darkness
they step willingly, their arms full of flowers

The crisis box *(for L)*

you send gifts: a red paper box
and a Chinese seal of stone, marked
with the ideograph for *crisis*

danger and opportunity, two sides
of the same moment

you send a letter
and a poem I wrote when I was fourteen
how we argued about evil then
ticking off the century's long list
until the air
                        turned sour

you said you wanted suffering
to be simple
                        that death was simple

***

you know there is no meaning
to history or philosophy

now that you are entering
this hoop of fire,
                                 memory

facing whatever you might find
armed with your small hands, tender skin

***

how can we know
the body without words
the heart in its black cave
underground
                    the blood circling
circling the labyrinth
searching for an opening
                                    wanting out

whatever nameless hand has touched
and tortured you
                         is here

you open the locks, bear
memory as a woman
bears a child

***

the polished marble seal
slender and cold
ink pad in its round gold case

you do not send the sign of happiness,
good luck, long life

you send the sign of crisis
in red, like a glass fire box

to be broken open

to sound the alarm

***

what kind of vampire
was stalking you
those years we gossiped
on the playground swings

I never saw him
                    merely felt
his cape at times
                    a shiver
someone walking
on my grave

you picked a strawberry, a daisy
all you wanted was to want
without complication

***

I close the crisis box
thinking of Pandora street
walking with you in the winter
how you bared your head
and let the rain fall down

how you interpreted my dreams
I was afraid
            you said

***

are there monsters in this world
or only illness

                    does it matter
what I call it
does it stop the screaming
in the nerves and muscles
shadow
          of the master
as he turns his back

***

a childish poem
the blank walls of this room

on the window sill, the crisis box
tied with a white string

***

and if I were to open up
that window, what would enter
air, a bird
             in the house

or would I step through to stand
outside
          and wash my hair with you again
in the dangerous rain

A misunderstanding

it's always something at this time
of the month keeping me awake, and tonight
it's a woman in a red dress and high heels
lying with her head against the curb outside my window
bleached hair in the gutter like new-threshed wheat
arms spread out like two limp jacket sleeves
before the jacket's sewn together
long neck the colour of straw thrown back
and flopping like the neck of a stuffed doll
kind of stupid, lolling like a drunk, one leg
coiled beneath her body, and the man
is trying to tell her something urgently
sitting on her chest, fist tearing the cheek
open in the bright circle of the street lamp
I can see the face striped with dirt
and a long ribbon of blood and she just
lies there while he keeps asking *don't you*
understand? don't you understand?

The mugging

The man who has been beaten lies sleeping,
one half of his face turned toward the light
from the hospital window. This is the half you see
as you enter: the loose purple casing
of skin like another man's skin pulled down
over his own, the slit bubble of the eyelid,
raw patch at the temple like a red coin.
Carelessly, they have left one hand intact,
and this is how you recognize him.

You cannot see into those sealed-up
places where the skin folds back on itself
and enters the body, dark locked muscle
of the throat, artery and clavicle
and lung, the brain in its blind, round bone.
The careless ones know more than you do;
they have reached the core of things, while your own
hands merely skimmed the surface, left no trace.
You can hear them boasting of their wisdom
in the streets below you, nothing to do
with politics or history, but with
who can touch this man most deeply. There are
flowers in the room, unbruised and yellow
petals opening as if to welcome
some newborn thing. You look at the one
familiar hand and wonder what it might
remember, what it might desire, what
might be restored to you.

The rescue

running on the river bank
everything green and rustling with fear
dark heat and the breathless
shadow of my body on the mud
running down the home street
past the houses of heart attack,
crohn's disease, muscular dystrophy
and drowning remember jessica
the girl in the well how all the united states
pulled her up out of that hole
reading her story in a dirty restaurant
two years later thinking why couldn't they
pull you up too why not you

and shall I say that you were tall
that you were sorrowful that you drank wine
with me, or that you saved my life
one night, this one I'm living now
sun lemons freckles hornets sugar
and this neck I carry
with such vanity, so much ingratitude
and shall I say I'm sorry
shall I say that I will walk
across the winter for you I will dive
beneath the ocean I will look for you
until the moon unravels
like a ball of wool, thin filaments
of memory spinning
everywhere

September

out here the air is sweet and orange and going to seed
it reeks of pumpkins, demoralized scarecrows
the sunflower bows its seedless head

four wasps are drowning, slowly
in a barrel of chokecherries; they make no sound
the school bus turns a corner, my child in its yellow maw

her father believes that I am practising
the occult arts of womanhood in his backyard
hatching great plots of clumsiness and mutability

but I am watching the eight wasps
gorging and sucking and smothering themselves
they quiver with pleasure

the neighbours believe that I am planning next year's garden
they imagine my head full of marigolds, snowpeas
but I am watching the nine wasps

now there are ten, drunk and striped
and stumbling deep among the berries
like babies falling asleep at play

the mailman thinks that I am waiting for him
"what are you doing today?" he asks, and I say, "nothing"
he hands me a letter with a foreign stamp

winter won't come to them, these twelve terrible wasps
I open your letter and a fine spray of dried petals
blows across the yard

Memoranda

Monday

Vijayan tells her, really, one day you must come to Singapore. One day you must visit India.

She sips her tea and says, I couldn't . . . *vacation* . . . where the people are so poor . . . the beggars.

By mistake, I write your name on a piece of paper and place it into the wrong pigeon hole.

Enclosed please find a copy of the copy you sent me.
A sentence you wrote in your sleep.

Vijay says, what are you talking about? There is not a day goes by, when I walk from my rooms to the university, that someone does not ask me for money.

Tuesday

At the bank, I reach for a deposit slip. A note on the back says: this is a holed up.

The man with the newspapers is sleeping in the library again.

The leaves turn yellow. Such a simple sentence.

Wednesday

The first time you saw me you said my name
was too difficult to spell.

You said you don't like to make mistakes.

I am sitting in a carrel by the window, watching the wind
strip leaves from the branches.

I am writing to tell you that I saw a sign on the Alberta
highway: Obey All Signs.

Thursday

The man with the newspapers carries his bundle
across campus like a mailman.

Like a letter I won't sign.

He is folding and unfolding. He makes a nest
of newsprint under the hydrangea.

A woman leaves the cafeteria and waits outside,
rubbing her own shoulders.

She picks at a flower and shivers.

I am forgetting that you touched me.

Friday

Vijay holds a lemon in his dark left hand.

I am sending you a memo: disregard all previous memos.

I am correcting my heart.

It stands corrected.

August, 1990

It was the summer of the Indian barricades.

I was looking at things.

The webs in the windowsills filled and overflowed with desiccated houseflies, the soft bodies of moths.

We were woken by thunder. We lay in our beds, sweating, scratching at mosquito bites.

The lightning crashed, continuous, till we could see the garden, clear as day.

I went to Ottawa and looked at the limestone.

I looked at the empty chairs. I think they are covered in velvet. If I could have touched them, I could tell you with certainty.

It is best to be precise.

You went to Lake Winnipeg to pick chokecherries and came back with a red rash that spread over your shoulder blades like wings.

Why did you not notice that the morning glory vines were strangling the bean plants, that the cucumbers were rusty?

It is easy to become lost and to misplace things.

It is easy to guess, to tell lies, to hallucinate.

With two sticks and a knot of white string, I built a cross. I dressed it in a cap and a shirt. The birds gathered, curious.

All summer we listened to rumours.

We placed green tomatoes in the sun and then forgot about them.

Our dreams were vivid as television.

In the evenings, there were vigils on the Legislature lawns.

The wind blew out our candles, one by one.

Children climbed up on Queen Victoria and looked into her stone eyes.

By the end of the month, the house was buried under drifts of dust.

The louder the drums sounded, the deeper we slept.

Squirrels tunnelled through to their nests in the attic.

And believing myself to be free of debt, I stood in the garden, smoking tobacco.

I breathe it in to me, watching the summer close.

The corn's bleached on the stalks; the peas rattle, brittle and bitter in their cold, white cages.

I am obedient, grammatical.

In fact, there is virtually nothing about me that is not controlled.

13 February *

while you, my friends, were knotting thick ropes
into nooses, letting your lungs fill up with water,
drinking whisky till your brains burst, I grew up,
paid taxes, wrote all your elegies for you and now
I am alive I am the one listening to the long
argument about the bomb shelter and whose fault
it was or was it an accident, listening
to the one side and the other and now glory glory glory
they are carrying out the stretchers for me
with the caved-in heads and the small heads
of ash, black and crinkled like balls of burnt paper
and I am an adult now I have paid for this, this
is the work I have contracted out, my dead friends, this
is what I have survived for: to see the strength and
brilliance of these crimes, to listen
to the long report, the long excuse, the endless
shift and shift of blame and
this is such an old story
see how it limps toward the end of the century
but it won't die

one father says that he will have justice
if it takes ten generations
and I might as well live
to see this thing done too

I want to live

as long as a stone lives
and
as
quietly

* On 13 February, 1991, the Canadian press reported that American forces had bombed a bomb shelter in Iraq, killing 500 civilians, mostly women and children, who were sleeping inside. Most of the dead were incinerated on contact. The image of their charred bodies being carried out into a crowd of weeping men was shown once or twice on television. Then it disappeared.

14 February

this morning I bought three helium balloons
at the Safeway: red, white, pink
with little hearts on their stretched cheeks
in the cold air, their skins puckered and dipped
and all the way home the February wind
battered their shrivelled faces against my coat

everything looks like a head to me now

George plunges his fists into the round, raw brain
of sourdough, and all afternoon it rises and swells

under their wet paper towels, the geranium seeds
believe it is spring; there is something that touches
plants and bread and these three coloured globes
expanding with warmth, tight and shiny and whole

the radio is the one tin thing in the room,
speaking of splintered skulls and the difficulty
of laying to rest so many children

my skeleton fidgets, jealous under the flesh
it wants to be touched too
and to be resurrected

Penance

On Quadra Island, Ellen bends over a drawing with her son.
This is a gift: the white crackle of paper, two pencils
leaving their traces, a sailboat, waves, a soft
grey smudge like a gull at the top
of the sky from where it sees Vijayan reading
a new poem to his new wife in Singapore,
a poem composed in blue ink on blue
airmail paper, translucent, barely visible. It is a song of
flight, exoneration. And Anne Marie hears it
spilling out into the valley of the rainforest
where she raises her camera, the sky tilts green.
The lens reflects her prayers, each one
a lush jewel strung on a clear thread, a promise
that this beauty will not lose its name, but rise again.
The trees shed their dappled shade, listening.
David is playing go; stones click across wood.
The go board blossoms with patterns: the double
eye at the centre, luminous and balanced,
the necessary breathing space, out of which he plucks
the cool bright discs, letting them slide
against each other in his hand. He says,
Yuriko is speaking of botanical gardens
in a Beijing classroom. Her students are dreaming
of lovers, of plum trees in bloom, of the intricate
brushstrokes that mean *a rose* and her heart
remembers suddenly a soft grey bird
above the Passage, remembers
a night in Sweden, snow descending
slowly over the white, dark villages
and the house where Lubomyr guides his fingers
over piano keys, black and white and smooth
as go stones, notes everywhere ascending
and surrounding his two small daughters
like drops of melting glass, a curtain
of rain. And Ellen carries

her sleeping boy up to his room.
She touches his body, the round scar on his back
where the miracle occurred, the pencil smudge
on his cheek like two soft wings
spread beside his smiling lips,
a testimony: the world moves into healing once
in a while. Our children fly toward us
on the night wind, their arms open and asking
that we bear witness to this.

Elegy

reading the story of the boy who died for seven
minutes, how he spoke of tunnels and the light
so clear and warm he thought that he was flying
how he saw the doctors open up his chest
he watched them from the ceiling
as if there could be ceilings up in heaven
or in hell
                    and in the bar tonight Blake says
it doesn't matter to him where he goes
cause he's got friends in both places
everybody laughs
                                        everybody tells stories

I was thinking of the rough, empty oceans of the moon
they are so dry
                                I was remembering the world for you
the winter caves beneath Niagara Falls
ice and fog like the cold breath of angels
the hollows that the sea makes
off Vancouver Island, three-toed tracks
of seabirds on the flat, dark sand
the sound of thunder as it rolls across the prairie
lightning on the green lake
                                                    you were wading
through the shallows, opening your mouth
to catch the rain; you said that nothing
ever tasted quite so simple
and invisible, that everything
comes down again to earth
                                                    as if surrendering

I heard many stories of descent,
growing up among Christians and Jews
they said you have to open your hands and receive
whatever is given to you; I admit there were times I envied
their faith, though I could see their hands were empty
I wanted the world to be other than what it is, wanted
its beaches and gardens to be places we could leave
and then return to
                                        as the moon returns at morning,
resting its pale, pocked face against the hills
I tell the children there is nothing
to be frightened of, but what do I know?
can I walk across the Redwood bridge,
as Rilke walked the parapet above the cliffs,
and hear the voices of the wind?
                                                                  I am like the conjurer
in the joke that Freud told: *can you summon spirits?*
asked the king, and the magician answered *yes,*
at your majesty's command, but they don't come

and what would Freud say of the boy who sailed
into that tunnel? it's true, the story sounds
a little like a birth: in a moment of emergency
the surgeon reaches in
and lifts out
                          the child's heart
he holds it gently, though he cannot say
what he is holding, what has broken free
it rests there in its cage of fingers,
forgets the body, forgets the mother, the songs it knew
it has never seen this light before

my niece is dancing on the lawn beneath the crooked oak
arms a perfect circle, brown hair streaming out around her
like the wings of a hummingbird in flight
she spins on her bare toes
                                        into invisibility
and back again and laughs as though the dance
were somehow ordinary,
                                      not a miracle
and I don't want to struggle
with this grieving any more; I want to think
about that small heart coming home
after its travels, how it began to beat again
I want to think about the messages
you used to send, how they flew
across the country, winter after winter,
the air above the desert thick and white
with envelopes
                         like snow

Michael Olito – Artist Biography

I am a visual artist who, of late, has been forced into the high-pressure, real world of big business and federal politics.

My early work concentrated on drawing, collage, and assemblages of found objects, natural materials, photographs, and written texts. Then came a move to conceptual and performance art that grew into collective pieces involving audience participation in huge, site-specific installations over extended periods of time. With the development of these "Ritual Deurbanization" pieces came a growing sense of social and political awareness. This culminated in last year's response to massive government cutbacks in art funding, cutbacks that forced me to assume the persona of The Flight Commander and enter into a form of public theatre of protest. As an alternative to the government's proposed purchase of billions of dollars of new helicopters, I developed the relatively inexpensive M.O./93–P.A.G. helicopter prototype which I demonstrated in Winnipeg and Ottawa and then attempted to sell to the Defence Department. Their lack of response to my proposal then forced me to run for parliament as a rogue member of the Rhinoceros party in an attempt to replace the government with a truly responsible one.